Circus World Muse~~presents~~

TRAINS OF THE CIRCUS
1872 THROUGH 1956

Fred Dahlinger, Jr.

Iconografix

Iconografix
PO Box 446
Hudson, Wisconsin 54016 USA

Iconografix books are offered at a discount when sold in quantity for promotional use. Businesses or organizations seeking details should write to the Marketing Department, Iconografix, at the above address.

Library of Congress Card Number: 99-76045

ISBN 1-58388-024-0

03 04 05 06 07 08 09 6 5 4 3 2

Printed in the United States of America

Cover and book design by Shawn Glidden

Copy editing by Dylan Frautschi

Iconografix Inc. exists to preserve history through the publication of notable photographic archives and the list of titles under the Iconografix imprint is constantly growing. Transportation enthusiasts should be on the Iconografix mailing list and are invited to write and ask for a catalog, free of charge.

Authors and editors in the field of transportation history are invited to contact the Editorial Department at Iconografix, Inc., PO Box 446/Dept. A-BK, Hudson, WI 54016. We require a minimum of 120 photographs per subject. We prefer subjects narrow in focus, e.g., a specific model, railroad, or racing venue. Photographs must be of high quality, suited to large format reproduction.

To Mom,
with love.

The circus train brought a self-contained city of thrilling entertainment and exciting education into every community it visited. This panoramic view shows a few of the 94 cars that transported the gigantic Ringling Bros. and Barnum & Bailey Combined Shows in 1920, along with the major tents that comprised the canvas city. The dining top is at the left front, with three baggage horse tops in the background. The midway area, with ticket wagons and concession stands, is on the right, in front of the sideshow bannerline. Behind the three-pole sideshow top

is the larger six-pole menagerie, entered via the marquee at the left end of the midway. In the background is the dominant eight-pole big top that measured 200 feet wide and 620 feet long. Inside its canvas confines over 15,000 people could be seated to enjoy each of the twice a day performances. With its three rings and four stages, this was the grandest circus that the world had ever seen, brought to town on the largest circus train then in operation. *Photograph by F. Meiner, June 7, 1920, Cleveland, Ohio, Circus World Museum.*

INTRODUCTION

A circus was presented before an American audience for the first time on April 4, 1793. It consisted of a program of horsemanship, rope walking, clowning, and ground acrobatics organized by John Bill Ricketts and presented within a ring. His troupe, and those that followed in the next three decades, erected temporary wood and canvas amphitheaters in major cities, where they played extended engagements. A portable canvas tent, or "pavilion," to house the performance, first used in 1825 by J. Purdy Brown, enabled a circus to relocate to a new community on a daily basis. Moving their baggage and personnel across land by horse, wagon and carriage, overland circuses erected their canvas "tops" in nearly every community encountered by their perambulating caravans. Coastal sailing vessels moved troupes in 1793 and other showmen visited inland river communities by steamboat commencing in 1822, but it was the nationwide network of railroads that eventually proved most adept in taking the circus to entertainment-seeking American audiences.

Show personnel, as a group, traveled by system passenger train in 1838. Soon after there was adequate trackage to do so, some circuses infrequently loaded their equipment onto leased system cars and made long-distance "jumps." In the 1850s and 1860s, the phrase "railroad circus" was used in a derogatory way. It defined a limited circus that consisted of only a big top show and a free attraction in the form of a limited parade or balloon ascension. It was "gillied" by hand labor and horse-drawn dray wagons from leased railroad cars to the appointed show grounds.

The stupendous success of the unprecedented P. T. Barnum Great Traveling World's Fair of 1871, the largest overland circus ever conceived, initiated the expansion of the genre into a large national enterprise. Faced with high expenses and low profits in small towns in 1871, the visionary Barnum suggested placing the show on rails in 1872. Thereby it would literally roll past small communities in favor of larger cities where greater net revenues could be realized. Partner Dan Castello, an experienced performer and show proprietor, who had perhaps the most experience with railroads of any showman, may have been against the idea. Another partner, W. C. Coup, is credited with solving the logistical problems in converting the Barnum circus into a successful railroad operation. Together these men rewrote the definition of a "railroad circus" to be a complete, large-scale operation that featured a big top show,

an expansive menagerie, and a sideshow or museum; all of it announced locally on "Circus Day" by a grand free street parade of impressive proportions and lengthy duration. The circus was really a regional enterprise until the epoch making 1872 Barnum railer. Within two seasons it had visited twenty-three of the thirty-seven states in the Union.

After starting the 1872 tour on a motley conglomeration of leased system cars, Coup realized that they needed to buy their own specialized cars. The first railroad cars of conventional design built for circus use were ordered by Coup for the 1872 Barnum show. Their acquisitions included flat cars for the baggage, parade, and cage wagons, and palace stock cars for elephants, horses, and lead stock. System coaches and sleeping cars, outfitted with high density bunk and compartment accommodations, conveyed the personnel. The railroad on which the circus traveled supplied the tracks, locomotives, caboose, and crew to move the special show train. The conversion from overland operation to their own train doubled the partners' invested capital to approximately $200,000, but in 1872 the Barnum circus grossed over a million dollars, the first to ever reach that mark. The net profits were $200,000, giving the partners a 100% return on their investment. By 1880 all of the leading American circuses were railroad shows. Proprietors that could not afford the purchase of a train of cars leased them.

Because show movement charges were based on the number of cars, instead of tonnage or length, circuses purchased and used extra long rolling stock to minimize their transportation expenses. Initially about 30 to 35 feet long, circus cars were 45 to 50 feet by the late-1870s and reached 60 feet by the early 1880s. The cars were 50 to 100 percent longer than similar system cars and were usually advertised as "double length" to convey grander proportions. The carrying capacity was 20,000 pounds in the mid-1870s and 30,000 by 1877. Some cars held 45,000-pound loads in the mid-1880s, 60,000 pounds was reached in the 1890s, and the first 80,000-pound cars were ordered about 1901-1902.

Wood construction prevailed until the first conventional steel cars were fabricated for traveling shows in 1911. Their higher, initial cost, coupled with the satisfactory use of existing wood cars, caused showmen to defer the purchase of steel cars until their old cars wore out or the railroads compelled them to upgrade their trains. The improved steel technology supported an increase to 70-foot cars in 1920 and 72-foot cars in 1928, along with an increase to 100,000-pound capacity by 1927. By 1929 all of the major circuses had finally converted to steel cars.

Circuses ordered their elephant, stock, and flat cars from ordinary railroad car builders. Recent studies have shown that about four dozen different fabricators furnished show cars. Builder identification of wood cars remains to be determined. The J. M. Gill Car Company, Barney & Smith Car Company, and Mt. Vernon Car Manufacturing Company appear to have been the principal builders of wood show cars. Post-1920 contributions by makers such as Mt. Vernon, Haffner-Thrall Car Co., and Warren Tank Car Company are well known and documented. The total contributions of the various American Car & Foundry Company plants remain to be assessed. Lease firms involved in the furnishing of show cars include the United States Rolling Stock Company, Venice Transportation Company, and the Arms Palace Horse Car Company.

In the heyday of the railroad circus, "Circus Day" was a local holiday equivalent to the 4th of July or Christmas. In most communities, it provided a day of respite in lives otherwise filled with the daily drudgery of work. The number of American circuses reached a zenith about 1905, when 100 independent troupes toured the states. Of these, the largest twenty-seven were railroad operations. Though they dominated the business, throughout the 1910s to 1930s competition from alternative entertainment caused a retrenchment in the number of circuses. The business reached an apparent nadir in 1938, but a short-lived mini-boom in railroad circuses occurred just as World War II came to a close. Escalation of costs and difficulties with a transient labor force finally caused the demise of the last two railroad-based tent circuses in 1956.

The photography reproduced in this book reflects the relatively limited number of circus train views, particularly of pre-1910 wood cars. While there are literally tens of thousands of conventional railroad photographs, precious few were ever made of circus trains. Show trains were typically parked and unloaded in a freight yard, a location not frequented by citizens unless there was a specific reason to be there. For most people, the glamorous part of the circus was the action in the streets or under the tents, not in the train yards. The physical action that took place there, unloading and loading, often in poor or little natural light early in the morning or late at night, challenged the photographic technology then available.

The illustrations herein include the earliest known photographs of most types of circus cars. These are the flat car (1872); advertising car (1876); elephant car (1880); stock car (1880); sleeping car (1886); and private car (1888). A few specialized types of cars, such as Adam Forepaugh's oil and trunk car and flats adapted to haul the mounted skin of Jumbo the elephant, or telescoping tableau wagons, remain to be discovered in photography.

The illustration arrangement is intended to trace the development of car design. While the order of the prints is generally chronological, some are inserted by the date of the car's manufacture, as opposed to the date of the photograph. In some cases suitable prints of cars in circus service have not been found. For those we have substituted clear shots of the cars while in later use on railroad carnivals.

RINGLING BROS. AND BARNUM & BAILEY, THE GREATEST SHOW ON EARTH, HAGENBECK-WALLACE and SELLS-FLOTO are trademarks and service marks of Ringling Bros. and Barnum & Bailey Combined Shows, Inc. Photographs containing these titles are reproduced with the permission of Ringling Bros. and Barnum & Bailey Combined Shows, Inc.

It has been my pleasure to receive the support of numerous individuals during the preparation of this book. Special appreciation is extended to Ray W. Buhrmaster, Jim Caldwell, Robert S. MacDougall, Fred D. Pfening, Jr., and Howard C. Tibbals for their assistance. Others who freely contributed of their knowledge include Gene Baxter, Joseph T. Bradbury, Albert Conover, Ron D. Goldfeder, John E. Gruber, Richard R. Goddard, Ed Hawkins, Paul Horsman, Doug Konkle, Fred D. Pfening III, Richard J. Reynolds III, William L. Rhodes, and Gregory P. Ames, Curator of the John W. Barriger III National Railroad Library. A note of gratitude is also due my colleagues at Circus World Museum: Harold Burdick, Erin Foley, Greg Parkinson, Tim Perkins, and Bernice Zimmer.

Fred Dahlinger, Jr.
Baraboo, Wisconsin
February 25, 2000

The first railroad show to incorporate all the features of a large overland circus was the P. T. Barnum Great Traveling World's Fair of 1872. The approximately 30-foot long flat cars on the right were specially fabricated for the show by the J.M. Gill Car Company of Columbus, Ohio. *Card photograph by Morris H. Porter, October 24, 1872, Kalamazoo, Michigan, Circus World Museum.*

The first circus advertising car was put on tour by P. T. Barnum's Greatest Show on Earth in 1876. The flamboyant owner's portrait and fine scenic paintings made a striking moving billboard as the car rolled along with the fast express trains to which it was attached. *Stereoview by J. A. French, Keene, circa 1876, New Hampshire, Richard W. Flint Collection.*

Before he became one of P. T. Barnum's partners in 1881, James A. Bailey was in a partnership with James E. Cooper. Their 1880 Great London Circus was the first to operate two advertising cars. Early Circus advertising cars were specially made for the service, but later cars were adaptations of older system cars. *Photograph, 1880, J. G. Brill Co. Collection, Mss 1556, #132, The Historical Society of Pennsylvania.*

Scenic paintings of the Great London Circus trains and the show's featured elephant acts filled one side of the 60-foot No. 1 Advertising Car. The show's original advance car, which became the first No. 2 car, was the prototype on which it was based. *Photograph, 1880, J. G. Brill Co. Collection, Mss 1556, #133, The Historical Society of Pennsylvania.*

The oversized Great London Circus elephant car measured about 46 feet long. Special attention was given to the design of the car's dual doors and ventilation openings to assure that the sensitive beasts inside would not be exposed to excessive drafts. *Photograph, 1880, J. G. Brill Co. Collection, Mss 1556, #135, The Historical Society of Pennsylvania.*

The wood frame and side truss, along with metal truss rods underneath the frame, typified circus car construction until the 1920s. An attractive three or four-color paint scheme was tastefully employed on this 50-foot Great London Circus vehicle. *Photograph, 1880, J. G. Brill Co. Collection, Mss 1556, #134, The Historical Society of Pennsylvania.*

One of the 50-foot flat cars made for the Great London Circus was a "run car," identifiable by the hourglass-shaped "snubber post" attached to the middle of each side. The rope used to lower wagons from the car deck to the ground, by means of a pair of inclined planes called "runs," was wound around it. *Photograph, 1880, J. G. Brill Co. Collection, Mss 1556, #136, The Historical Society of Pennsylvania.*

W. W. Cole operated a medium-size railroad circus beginning in 1873, when he went to the west coast on a train of leased cars. At his retirement in 1886, Cole was one of the richest men in the circus business, the result of skillfully routing his circus into fresh territory. Though numbered No. 3, this relatively short advertising car was one of just two that traveled in advance of his circus. *Stereoview stamped R. D. Ryerson, 1883, Howard C. Tibbals Collection.*

The sleeping cars of the John B. Doris New Monster Shows included two converted coaches and a vintage baggage car for the workingmen. Other shows utilized modified box cars for sleeping accommodations and storage. *Stereoview by Kirk & Sayre, 1884, Huntington, West Virginia, Circus World Museum.*

Car No. 50 was the private car of James A. Bailey in 1888 and may have served the same purpose for James L. Hutchinson, another Barnum show partner, in 1886. It was later transformed into an advertising car for the Adam Forepaugh & Sells Brothers Shows Combined by 1898. *Card photograph by W. N. Sweet, 1888, Chicago, Illinois, Circus World Museum.*

With more than 60 cars, the 1889 Barnum & Bailey's Greatest Show on Earth train was divided into several parts, or "sections," each of which was loaded in a pre-planned, systematic manner. This section carried apparatus for the big top. *Card photograph, August 23, 1889, near Potsdam, New York, Howard C. Tibbals Collection.*

Six sleeping cars of the Wallace & Co.'s Great Shows represented several different makes of former system coaches and sleepers. Circuses refitted the interiors of these cars to suit their own purposes. Barely visible on the extreme right side, the seventh Wallace sleeper was a converted box car. *Photograph, circa 1890, Fred D. Pfening, Jr. Collection.*

The Mt. Vernon Car Manufacturing Company was a significant builder of both wood and steel frame show cars from its founding in 1890 until the late 1920s. The flat car made for the Richards 3 Big Shows Combined in 1890 or 1891 had exceptionally high sideboards, or "gunnels," a term derived from "gunwales" by showmen. *Photograph, John Robinson Circus Scrapbook, The Public Library of Cincinnati and Hamilton County.*

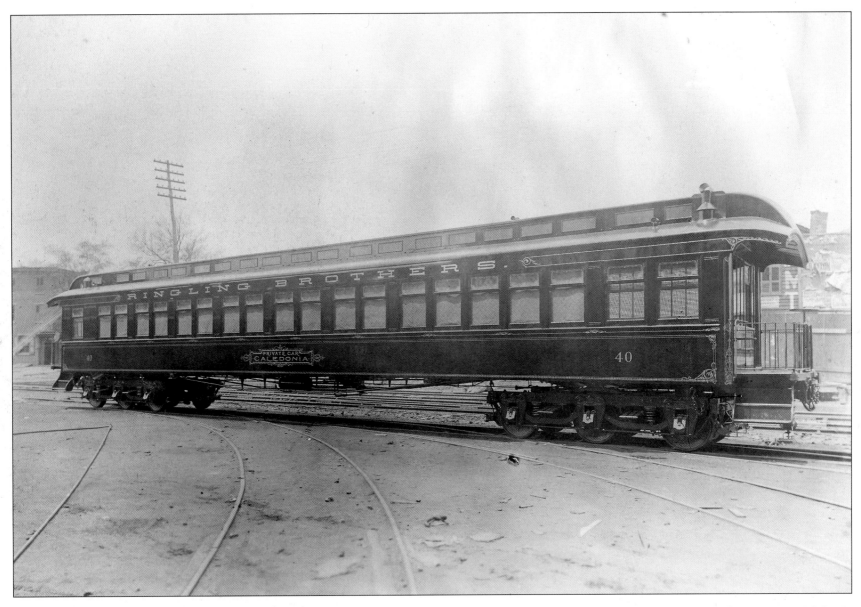

The five Ringling brothers bought their first private car, the "Caledonia," from Jackson & Sharp in 1892. It accompanied the circus cars of the Ringling Bros.' World's Greatest Shows as they aggressively expanded their playing territory in the 1890s. *Print from original negative, 1892, Jackson & Sharp Collection, Delaware State Archives.*

The Ringlings operated four advertising cars as early as 1892, testimony to the importance of the advance to a circus. Car No. 4 was nicknamed "The War Eagle." The "Warriors" who traveled in this "brigade" car were charged with protecting the show's lithographs from competing circus billposters. *Card photograph, circa 1892, Circus World Museum.*

One string, or "cut," of Ringling Bros. flats has already been unloaded and another awaits attention from the train crew. The many fine Asiatic elephants of the show have departed their cars and have just commenced their ritual trek to the show grounds. *Print from original negative, circa 1894, Frank F. Foster Collection, State Historical Society of Iowa, Iowa City, Iowa.*

Vintage baggage cars from system railroads were converted into railroad circus advertising cars, giving them a second life. J. H. LaPearl's 1897 car proudly proclaimed the railroad nature of his show above the scenic panels on the car. *Card photograph by S. G. Wray & Co., 1897, Crawfordsville, Indiana, C. S. Primrose Collection, Circus World Museum.*

Several different types of traveling shows utilized a hybrid stock and flat car. This one, made for Evansville, Wisconsin, showman George W. "Popcorn" Hall by the Ohio Falls Car Company, hauled both wagons and exotic animals – probably camels or dromedaries and elephants. *Photograph, circa 1899, Jeffersonville, Indiana, William L. Rhodes Collection.*

The St. Charles, Missouri, plant of the American Car & Foundry Company (ACF) made this flat for the Grand Circo Orrin of Mexico City in March 1900. *Photograph, 1900, St. Charles, Missouri, John W. Barriger III National Railroad Library, St. Louis Mercantile Library, University of Missouri-St. Louis.*

An entirely different and more economical flat car design was furnished by ACF to Norris & Rowe's Big Trained Animal Shows in 1900. It had lower gunnels and lacked the side support posts of the Orrin car. *Photograph, 1900, St. Charles, Missouri, John W. Barriger III National Railroad Library, St. Louis Mercantile Library, University of Missouri-St. Louis.*

By the turn of the century some shows dropped scenic paintings on their advertising cars in favor of elaborate title schemes. One of the finest examples was with Sig. Sautelle's New Big Railroad Shows, a 1901-1903 operation. *Card photograph, circa 1901, Howard C. Tibbals Collection.*

The most traveled of advertising cars was the Barnum & Bailey vehicle that toured the United States in the 1890s and then Europe from 1898 to 1902. The lower cabinets stored large quantities of lithographs that were assembled into daily-posted bundles, called "hods," on the counters. Sleeping berths for crew members were hinged upwards, over the work areas. *Card photograph, 1900, probably Berlin, Germany, Circus World Museum.*

The train crew has set the runs on the second cut of Adam Forepaugh & Sells Bros. Shows flats. They then positioned the sawhorses, called "jacks," under the runs so that the ramps can support the great weight of the wagons passing over them. *Photograph, 1901, Circus World Museum.*

A steam calliope and seven "cross" cages totally filled one Great Pan American Shows flat car. To coordinate the lifting motions of the train crew in turning the short cages perpendicular to the length of the car, a boss would call out "raise her back." This was shortened to "razorbacks" and used to designate the men who loaded and unloaded the flats. *Print from original negative, 1902, Gift, Bert Chipman, Circus World Museum.*

The largest circuses provided handsomely appointed dining cars for the use of staff and performers. Fancy menus were printed for special occasions. This was the interior of a dining car in the Ringling Bros.' World's Greatest Shows train in about 1902. *Photograph, circa 1902, Charles Andress Scrapbook, Gift, Mrs. Charles (Virginia) Andress, Circus World Museum.*

A few circuses ventured into Colorado narrow gauge country, parking their standard gauge equipment and moving locally on cars leased from the railroad. The Gentry operation sent one of its dog and pony shows there about 1902. Locomotive 201, a 2-8-0 Consolidation-type, was furnished by the Grant Locomotive Works to the Denver and Rio Grande in 1881. *Photograph, circa 1902, Circus World Museum.*

The Skerbeck family of Dorchester, Wisconsin, hauled their show in a pair of express-type cars furnished by the Burton Stock Car Company. Known as "two car shows," these compact outfits brought quality entertainment to smaller cities and towns adjacent to the rail lines. *Photograph, circa 1902, Ontonagon, Michigan, Mitch Gorrow Collection, Circus World Museum.*

The only circus advertising car ornamented with carvings was the No. 1 Advertising Car of the John Robinson Ten Big Shows. The 1903 decorations were finished by the Ohio Scroll & Lumber Company of Covington, Kentucky. *Photograph, 1903, John Robinson Collection, Cincinnati Museum Center Image Archives.*

Two fine African elephants, Mike and Topsy, were among the "bulls" that rode in this approximately 50-foot long Adam Forepaugh & Sells Bros. Shows elephant car. It was probably one of several made by John Gill for his hometown circus, owned by the four Sells brothers of Columbus, Ohio. *Print from original negative, circa 1902, Frederick W. Glasier Collection, John and Mable Ringling Museum of Art.*

The man on the left held the rope that restrained this stringer wagon as it descended the runs. This Forepaugh-Sells flat car was built by the Gill firm several decades before the scene was photographed. *Photograph, circa 1903, Fred D. Pfening, Jr. Collection.*

By 1905 the Ringlings reached the top of the circus world and battled James A. Bailey for supremacy. Their advance efforts took place from several railroad advertising cars, including this attractively titled No. 1 car. *Card photograph by Vreeland, 1905, Enid, Oklahoma Territory, Richard W. Flint Collection.*

The ornate interior of the circa-1905 Sells-Floto Circus advertising car glistened, the woodwork heavily varnished and the brass work polished to a high gleam. The boys relaxed for their photograph before hustling to get more lithographs posted on buildings and walls, and in windows. *Photograph, circa 1905, Circus World Museum.*

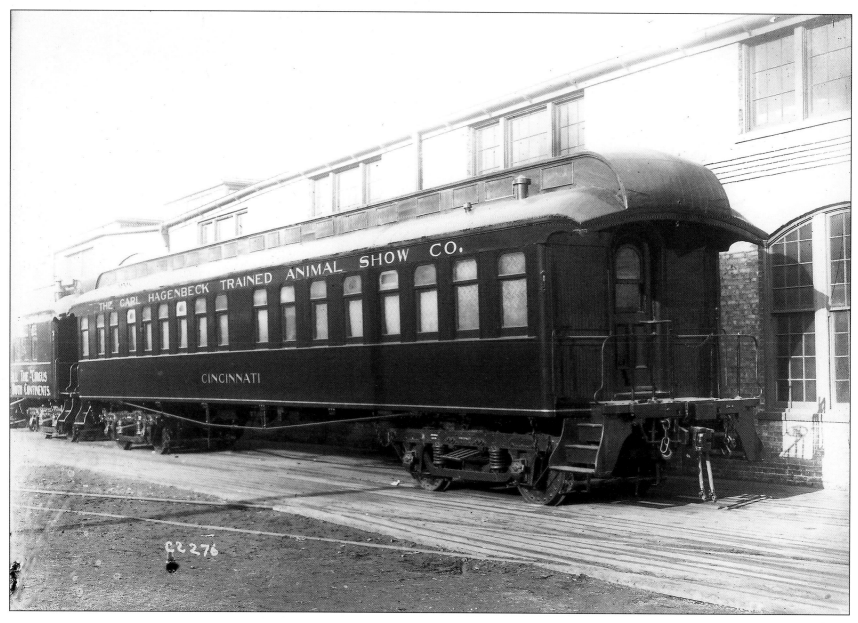

The entirely new Carl Hagenbeck Trained Wild Animal Show Co. of 1905 bought its sleeping cars from the Pullman Company. This car, named for the city that served as the show's base of operations, may have been the rolling home of the show owners or managers. *Photograph, 1905, Pullman, Illinois, Smithsonian Institution.*

The five Gollmar brothers were first cousins to the Ringling brothers. They operated a medium-sized railroad circus from 1903 through 1916. The Gollmar advance crew posed proudly beside the car that was their traveling home from April through October. *Card photograph, circa 1906, Gift, Robert H. Gollmar, Circus World Museum.*

The white-jacketed men may have been the porters that staffed the sleeping car in the background. As sleeping car companies and railroads sold off their older cars, like this narrow vestibule car, circuses updated their own rolling stock. *Card photograph, circa 1906, Circus World Museum.*

Circus advertising cars were moved from city to city by coupling them to regularly scheduled passenger trains. Norris & Rowe Circus Advertising Car No. 3 was headed for the next city to be billed by the crew. *Photograph by Brown Bros., circa 1908, Howard C. Tibbals Collection.*

Two strings of baggage horse cars have been parked and unloading has commenced, while a switch engine spotted the first cut of flat cars to be unloaded. The stock car roofs were fitted with bins to store spare wood planks, seat stringers, and poles. *Photograph, 1908, Philadelphia, Pennsylvania, Circus World Museum.*

The morning air was cool when the Barnum & Bailey crew went about unloading a cut of flats. At least three two-horse pull over teams assured that the wagons moved constantly along the flats and down the runs. *Print from original negative, 1908, Keeneland, Lexington, Kentucky, Keeneland-Cook Collection.*

All of the technology that was perfected by circuses for the rapid unloading of wagons from flat cars can be seen in this photograph. With it, the Barnum & Bailey razorbacks made easy work of unloading the more than 30 flats that hauled the show. *Photograph, circa 1908, Circus World Museum.*

During a long trip, or "jump," circuses scheduled stops to feed and water the animals. The fancy carved sideboards of the Barnum & Bailey tableau cages were removed so that the keepers could tend to their charges. *Postcard photograph, circa 1908, Circus World Museum.*

Known mostly for overland operations, Mollie A. Bailey put a four-car show on rails in 1907 and two years later acquired this baggage car from the Southern Iron & Equipment Company. *Photograph, July 12, 1909, Atlanta, Georgia, Ray W. Buhrmaster Collection.*

Rarely was the night loading of a circus captured on film. Here's an unusual view of the Barnum & Bailey show baggage stock being loaded into their cars. Wood cars were intentionally built with the longitudinal arch visible here. *Photograph by Underwood & Underwood, circa 1909, Howard C. Tibbals Collection.*

Many circuses leased cars to minimize their capital investment. The Venice Transportation Company was the leading rental firm of the early 1900s. They provided a complete train of 50,000-pound capacity stocks and flats, 60-feet long, to handle the Great Sells-Floto Circuses Consolidated. *Print from original negative by Charles Puck, circa 1909, Circus World Museum.*

Venice-built stock cars had a distinctive design that exposed the uprights of the side trusses through the side sheathing. The truss rods that handled the tension loads in wood-framed cars can be clearly seen. *Photograph, September 16, 1915, Havensville, Kansas, Circus World Museum.*

John H. Sparks expanded his three-car show, which included the nearly 80-foot long end-loading car on the right, with the purchase of a stock and flat from Mt. Vernon. The Sparks operation quickly grew into a fine 15-car rail show in the 1910s. *Photograph, circa 1909, Howard C. Tibbals Collection.*

Winter was still present in Baraboo, Wisconsin, as the bull men supervised the first loading of the elephants into their cars. A number of the local boys turned out to observe the annual early spring ritual that took place near the Chicago & North Western Railway facility. *Postcard photograph, circa 1910, Baraboo, Wisconsin, Ralph D. Pierce Collection.*

Cuts of circus flats were not always parked on straight track. Here a Ringling poler carefully surveys the chocks obscuring the car deck as he steers lion cage #76 between the flat car gunnels. *Postcard photograph by H. W. Pelton, October 17, 1910, Asheville, North Carolina, Circus World Museum.*

Lead stock, including camels, zebras, and sacred cows rode in stock cars. Some of the camels that comprised the fancy parade hitch of the John Robinson's Ten Big Shows waited outside their car as others descend the ramp, termed a "run," by circus personnel. *Postcard photograph, circa 1910, Circus World Museum.*

The Ringling "bull" men stood on top of their dormitory on wheels, the end of an elephant car that was converted into a sleeping space. The men were housed close to their animals so that they could quickly reach them during feed stops and upon arrival for unloading. *Postcard photograph, circa 1910, Howard C. Tibbals Collection.*

The six or seven-car Bulger & Cheney Dog and Pony Shows traveled on a train of second-hand vehicles. A Burton stock headed the consist, followed by an Arms Palace Horse Car Company stock and three wood flats, perhaps all of them leased from William P. Hall, a circus broker in Lancaster, Missouri. *Photograph, 1911, Circus World Museum.*

The first conventional steel-frame cars built for a traveling show were furnished in 1911. They later became part of the Jones Bros. World Toured Shows in the mid-1910s, the first circus to have a complete train of steel cars. One of the Standard Steel Car Company stock cars was later owned by Dodson's Imperial Shows, a railroad carnival. *Photograph, circa 1949, Gene Baxter Collection.*

Distinctively shaped vertical stiffeners on the car sides were one way to identify the 60-foot Standard Steel Car Company flats that were fabricated in 1911. Steel flats like this Sheesley carnival vehicle hauled the Jones Bros. World Toured Shows in the mid-1910s. *Photograph by William H. B. Jones, 1939, Fred Heatley Collection.*

Fred B. Hutchinson and his daughter posed with his car "Hutch" on the 1912 Sells-Floto Circus. The use of private cars was limited to show owners and general managers, with staff and top performers receiving staterooms or compartments. *Print, 1912, Fred D. Pfening, Jr. Collection.*

Animal scenes, the show title, and a reference to the show's spectacle, "Cleopatra," were featured on the 1912 Barnum & Bailey Advertising Car No. 3. Simpler decorative schemes would return within a few years. *Card photograph by W. H. Woodhead, Fitchburg, Massachusetts, 1912, Fred D. Pfening, Jr. Collection.*

The Barnum & Bailey elephant keepers waited for the instruction to begin their walk to the show grounds. To the right of the three elephant cars was the show's seldom photographed boxcar, used to haul supplies, spare poles, and extra tent canvas. *Photograph by A. L. Chumley, October 13, 1913, Birmingham, Alabama, Circus World Museum.*

The "pie car" was a cafeteria on wheels where staff, performers, and working people could get coffee, sandwiches, pie, and other things to eat and drink after they boarded the show train. The interior of this Ringling pie car was decorated for Independence Day. *Photograph, circa 1913, Howard C. Tibbals Collection.*

Another of Sig Sautelle's attempts at owning a circus came in 1913. For that venture he acquired this flat car, presumably second hand, from the Southern Iron & Equipment Company. *Photograph, 1913, Atlanta, Georgia, Ray W. Buhrmaster Collection.*

The morning sunlight is evident in this view of Percheron horses leaving an Arms Palace Horse Car Company stock car. It was one of several leased to Fred Buchanan's Yankee Robinson Shows in the mid-1910s. A spare tent pole is stored on the car roof. *Photograph, circa 1913, Circus World Museum.*

Even before the Ringling Bros.' World's Greatest Shows train came to a stop, the men of the circus were ready for the day's work. The horse men stood atop their cars and the razorbacks, the men who unloaded the flat cars, were stirring. Ten-wheeler No. 1738 was furnished by Brooks to the Union Pacific Railroad in 1899 and renumbered in 1915. *Photograph, circa 1914, Howard C. Tibbals Collection.*

Sells-Floto replaced their Venice flats with these 60-footers from another supplier by the time this photograph was taken. The paint scheme was likely white sides and red ends with lettering in red and blue. *Photograph, 1915, Fred D. Pfening, Jr. Collection.*

A vintage Keystone Palace Horse Car Company stock car, probably built by the Pullman Company, was used on the 1915 Barton & Bailey's Shows. Car leasing firms including Keystone, Burton, and Venice also sold a variety of cars to private users after removing them from revenue service. *Photograph, circa 1915, William P. Hall Papers, Circus World Museum.*

Baggage horses wore their collars and harness when they exited the horse cars. These are probably two Barney & Smith-built cars that have been well maintained. *Print from original negative by Charles Puck, 1918, Los Angeles, California, Circus World Museum.*

The Hagenbeck-Wallace Circus ordered the first full complement of new circus cars made with steel frames for the season of 1920. The contract for elephant, stock, and flat cars was filled by the Mt. Vernon Car Manufacturing Company. *Photograph by Karl K. Knecht, circa 1922, West Baden, Indiana, Circus World Museum.*

These distinctive straight-sided flats furnished by Mt. Vernon in 1920 apparently had a design deficiency and were replaced within a few years. The Mt. Vernon cars were 70-footers with a 60,000-pound load capacity. *Photograph by Karl K. Knecht, circa 1922, West Baden, Indiana, Circus World Museum.*

By April 1921, Mt. Vernon fabricated at least one flat with a "fish belly" side profile for Hagenbeck-Wallace. Here is such a vehicle serving as a run car, with the 1920 vintage straight-side flats awaiting unloading in the background. The new design increased car strength while improving access to the trucks. *Photograph, circa 1921, Earl Chapin May Collection, Circus World Museum.*

Mt. Vernon designed a second style of straight-sided flat car in 1921 and manufactured a few for railroad circus and carnival owner James Patterson in the 1920s. One of the Mt. Vernons later served on the Cole Bros. Circus from 1936 to 1949. *Photograph, 1942, Robert S. MacDougall Collection.*

The Howe's Great London Circus of 1921 was assembled from the best parts of two different circuses. The well-finished wagons rode across the rails on at least three different styles of wood flat cars. *Photograph, 1921, Circus World Museum.*

Andrew Downie bought several new 61-foot flat cars from the Haffner-Thrall Car Company in 1921 and 1922 for his Walter L. Main Circus. A number of Haffner-Thrall cars, with steel draft sills, were later used on railroad carnivals, such as Hennies Bros. Shows, in the 1940s. *Photograph by William Koford, 1942, Albert Conover Collection.*

Despite the fact that railroad men preferred to handle steel cars and that smaller shows had ordered them beginning in 1920, Ringling Bros. and Barnum & Bailey Combined Shows continued to travel on a fleet of well-maintained wood cars through the 1928 season. *Postcard photograph, 1921, Circus World Museum.*

The Warren Tank Car Company began fabricating show cars about 1909. Some of the flats they made for the Bernardi Greater Shows, with an external truss under the center sills, were later sold to Ringling Bros. and Barnum & Bailey Combined Shows. *Photograph, 1926, Warren, Pennsylvania, Howard C. Tibbals Collection.*

George Christy's three-car Christy Shows used an end-loading "tunnel" car to carry the show's low-profile canvas, baggage, and prop wagons. The techniques for loading and unloading were adapted from flat car operations. *Photograph, 1921, Circus World Museum.*

To haul the enormous male Asiatic elephant, "Tusko," Al G. Barnes ordered a unique drop frame elephant car from the Mt. Vernon Car Manufacturing Company for the 1922 season. With a raised roof over the center well, the car could readily accommodate the mammoth pachyderm. *Photograph by William H. B. Jones, September 29, 1934, Galveston, Texas, Robert S. MacDougall Collection.*

The Keith Railway Equipment Company, a Chicago car-leasing firm, supplied a train of nineteen elephant, stock, and flat cars to the 1922 Sells-Floto Circus. The elephant car and one stock car are shown here. Many Keith tank cars were fabricated by the American Car & Foundry Company. *Photograph, circa 1922, Gift, Robert Good, Circus World Museum.*

The flat cars supplied by Keith did not have as pronounced a "fish belly" drop as similar Mt. Vernon cars. All of the Sells-Floto cars were 70-foot long and carried an 80,000-pound capacity rating. *Postcard photograph, circa 1922, Gift, Walter F. Tyson, Circus World Museum.*

The sleepers utilized by the three large circuses of the American Circus Corporation had the show title painted on both the car sides and roof. Perhaps the idea was to enable viewers in airplanes to identify the circus. *Photograph by Karl K. Knecht, circa 1922, West Baden, Indiana, Circus World Museum.*

Occasionally a circus train passed some terrific scenery in daylight. Such was the case in the 1920s, when Ringling Bros. and Barnum & Bailey Combined Shows made several long distance western tours. The show coaches were photographed with beautiful Mt. Shasta in the background. *Photograph by Pete Mardo, circa 1923, near Mt. Shasta, California, Circus World Museum.*

The entire 29-car Al G. Barnes Circus train stopped on an undulating curve in 1924 to effect a wheel repair. Soon afterwards the three Southern Pacific Lines consolidation-style pushers coupled on to the caboose and helped to move the train over the grade to the next engagement. *Photograph by Walker Morris, September 28, 1924, near Weed, California, Joseph T. Bradbury Collection.*

The large three-track car shop at Ringling Bros. and Barnum & Bailey Combined Shows' winter quarters maintained a fleet of 100 railroad cars to haul the circus in the 1920s. The elephant, stock, and flat cars visible were probably built by Barney & Smith. *Photograph by Frank Updegrove, 1925, Bridgeport, Connecticut, Howard C. Tibbals Collection.*

Stock cars like this Mt. Vernon example were outfitted internally with special feeding troughs for baggage horses. Performing horses traveled in similar cars but were separated by pivoting barriers that created a stall for each individual animal. *Photograph, 1925, Howard C. Tibbals Collection.*

Elephant cars constructed by Mt. Vernon, as with Keith, had small sliding doors to readily control the flow of air into the interior. Two of the floor clean out doors of this Sparks World Famous Shows bull car are shown in a partially open position. *Photograph, circa 1925, Fred D. Pfening, Jr. Collection.*

Living space inside sleeping cars was at a premium. Bunks were two high and two across in this womens' car. Workingmens' sleepers had three high bunks and were notoriously hot during the summer, causing many men to ride the open flats. *Print from original negative by Harry A. Atwell, circa 1926, Circus World Museum.*

When the Barnum & Bailey and Ringling Bros. shows were merged for 1919, the best cars from both circuses were selected for further use. Baggage stock cars from both shows are visible in this 1926 view. *Print from original negative by Harry A. Atwell, 1926, Chicago, Illinois, Circus World Museum.*

The first steel frame car built for Ringling Bros. and Barnum & Bailey Combined Shows was this steel sheathed stock. It hauled "Pawah," a white elephant, with the show in 1927. RBBB replaced all of their wood, elephant, stock, box, and flat cars within the next two years. *Photograph, 1927, Warren, Pennsylvania, Howard C. Tibbals Collection.*

Among the first of the 100,000 pound-rated cars was this 70-foot flat for Floyd and Howard King's Walter L. Main Circus of 1927. Warren redesigned their flats to eliminate the truss arrangement under the center draft sills. *Photograph, 1927, Warren, Pennsylvania, Howard C. Tibbals Collection.*

Knickers were in style when this all-male crowd gathered to observe the unloading of the Hagenbeck-Wallace Circus. The snubber is getting his rope ready for the lowering of water wagon number 65, while teams of Percherons await their hauling duties on the right. *Photograph, 1927, Fred D. Pfening, Jr. Collection.*

A Hagenbeck-Wallace poler carefully steered wagon number 70 to the runs, where it will begin its descent to the ground. Experienced polers kept out in front of the wagon pole, in the event that a wheel obstruction caused the undergear to swing abruptly to the side. *Photograph, 1927, Fred D. Pfening, Jr. Collection.*

Some circuses, including Christy Bros., continued to travel with wood cars as late as Ringling-Barnum, but the railroads kept pressuring shows to convert to steel cars. Wood horse cars like this one survived only a few more years of service before being scrapped. *Photograph by John Cutler, August 3, 1927, Newport, Rhode Island, Edward F. Tracy, Jr. Collection.*

The queen of aerial gymnasts, Lillian Leitzel, and a young friend, Dolly John, enjoyed her commodious stateroom in a Ringling Bros. and Barnum & Bailey Combined Shows sleeper. It was outfitted with a piano, radio, cylinder music box, and other amenities from home. Only the premier performers ever received such treatment. *Print from original negative by Harry A. Atwell, circa 1928, Circus World Museum.*

The largest order ever placed for show cars was given by Ringling Bros. and Barnum & Bailey Combined Shows to the Warren Tank Car Company for the 1928 and 1929 seasons. This was one of the elephant cars they furnished, identifiable by the small size ventilation openings. *Photograph, 1940, Gift, Walter F. Tyson, Circus World Museum.*

This circa 1932 Ringling Bros. and Barnum & Bailey Combined Shows view shows the title boards in their original position, midway up the height of the car. These baggage horse cars were in the second of four sections that comprised 90 cars. *Photograph, circa 1932, Robert S. MacDougall Collection.*

The first section, known since the early 1900s as the "Flying Squadron," has just pulled into town on the new Warren flats. The Ringling Bros. and Barnum & Bailey Combined Shows flats are painted orange with the lettering in black. *Print from original negative by Tom Scaperlanda, October 1, 1928, San Antonio, Texas, Circus World Museum.*

The 15-car Gentry Bros. Circus of 1929 has been parked, or "spotted," at a good level crossing and the teams are ready to work. The stocks were new from the Warren Tank Car Company and the flats were the straight-sided Mt. Vernons of 1921 and 1924 vintage. *Photograph by S. Achber, July 26, 1929, Laconia, New Hampshire, Fred D. Pfening, Jr. Collection.*

The Sells-Floto circus leased three cars from Venice Transportation Company in 1929, two of which are illustrated here. The firm furnished three different styles of cars, one of which was a 70-foot, 80,000-pound capacity semi-steel type of car made that year. *Photograph, 1929, Gift, Michael D. Sporrer, Circus World Museum.*

It was unusual to have a former rail post office car utilized as a circus sleeper, but Al G. Barnes always sought bargains and perhaps this was one of them. The flamboyant lettering styles of the past superseded by shaded block lettering. *Photograph, 1930, Circus World Museum.*

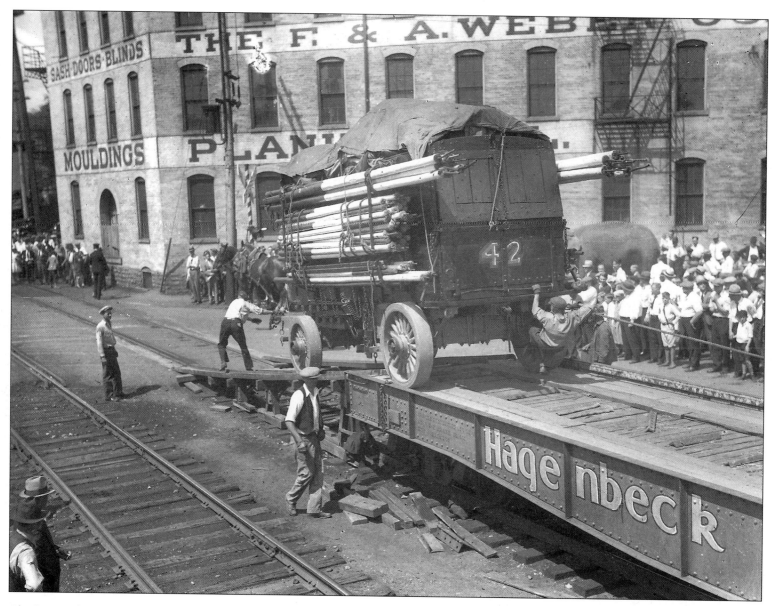

A classic shot of circus train action was captured on film during the unloading of the Hagenbeck-Wallace Circus. The poler is just about to leap out of the way of the descending wagon and the hook rope man has just grabbed a ride to make it easier to disengage the hook rope from the wagon. *Print from original negative by Harry A. Atwell, May 9, 1932, Cincinnati, Ohio, Circus World Museum.*

Four cuts of flats held the wagons of the 1932 Hagenbeck-Wallace Circus. The nearby men are probably seeking employment with the circus during tough depression-era times. *Photograph, June 5, 1932, Brooklyn, New York, Fred D. Pfening, Jr. Collection.*

The Mt. Vernon style of stock car construction is identifiable by the absence of diagonals in the end panels of the sides. This 72-foot stock car was built for the 1928 John Robinson Circus. *Photograph, 1933, Circus World Museum.*

When Sam Gumpertz assumed the management of Ringling Bros. and Barnum & Bailey Combined Shows for 1933, he changed the color scheme of the train. The flats of the show were painted aluminum and the word "Circus" replaced "Shows" in the title. These cuts were parked in the New Haven railroad yards before the spring opener. *Print from original negative by Gene Trexler, 1934, New York, New York, Circus World Museum.*

These two views form a panorama of the arrival and unloading of the Hagenbeck-Wallace and Forepaugh-Sells Combined Circus of 1935. The Chicago and North Western Railway hauled the show trains into town and the cuts were then spotted in the C&NW yards for unloading. A C&NW Class E-1 Pacific, number 2202, built in 1913 at Schenectady, New York, awaited its next passenger train assignment. *Photograph, September 1, 1935, Waukegan, Illinois, Fred D. Pfening, Jr. Collection.*

The crowd gathered at the crossing witnessed the unloading of one cut, along with the passage of the horses, lead stock, and elephants to the show grounds. Steam locomotive servicing facilities, a switch tower, and commuter train cars complete the scene. *Photograph, September 1, 1935, Waukegan, Illinois, Fred D. Pfening, Jr. Collection.*

A fine example of a brightly decorated advertising car was the one used by Ringling Bros. and Barnum & Bailey Combined Circus in the late 1920s and early 1930s. The white body and red title boards provided a suitable backdrop to the finely executed animal depictions. *Photograph by Koons, circa 1935, Sarasota, Florida, Howard C. Tibbals Collection.*

Show laborers earned their keep in the spring by repairing all of the show cars. These men are posed at work on the sleeper "Memphis" of the Cole Bros. World Toured Circus. *Print from original negative by Harry A. Atwell, 1936, Rochester, Indiana, Circus World Museum.*

The spring loading of another cage wagon was underway at the Ringling Bros. and Barnum & Bailey Combined Circus winter quarters. The horses dug in for a footing in the sandy soil, assisted by the poler, the rope guider, and the wheel chocker. *Photograph, circa 1937, Sarasota, Florida, Howard C. Tibbals Collection.*

The Al G. Barnes Circus bought Mt. Vernon cars in the 1920s, but a Keith car formerly with Sells-Floto was at the head end of this nicely painted set of flats that carried the Al G. Barnes and Sells-Floto Combined Circus title. The show's hippo den, one of the heaviest wagons ever constructed, is the first wagon. *Print from original negative by Charles Puck, March 17, 1937, Baldwin Park, California, Circus World Museum.*

When baggage stock were replaced by tractors at the outset of the 1938 season, Ringling Brothers and Barnum & Bailey Combined Shows utilized elephants for some of the tasks previously handled by the horses. Here a team of bulls is being used in pull over service, whereby one wagon is pulled from one flat over to another. *Photograph by Chester Photo Service, circa 1942, Circus World Museum.*

Nearly 60 cars can be seen in this view of the sidings at the Ringling Bros. and Barnum & Bailey Combined Shows winter quarters. Despite the difficulty of routing the circus train during World War II, the federally recognized need for entertainment assured continued operation. *Photograph, circa 1945, Sarasota, Florida, Circus World Museum.*

The Cole Bros. Circus train, one of only two rail shows to continue on tour during the war, passed over a viaduct on the way into the wheeling yards. The Cole show acquired its mix of flats from a number of defunct circuses and carnivals. *Print from original negative by John Wyatt, May 23, 1944, Wheeling, West Virginia, Howard C. Tibbals Collection.*

The approaching conclusion of the war spurred the formation of several new railroad circuses. One of the outfits was the Russell Bros. Pan-Pacific Circus, framed with Warren-built stocks and flats, and converted system coaches. *Print from original negative by Harry Quillen, 1945, Circus World Museum.*

The entire 17-car Clyde Beatty Circus train headed into town on the Union Pacific Railroad behind 2-10-2, number 5075, a Class TTT locomotive built at Lima, Ohio, in 1923. Smaller shows like this one traveled in just one section. *Photograph by Art Stensvad, July 13, 1947, North Platte, Nebraska, Gift, Paul van Pool, Circus World Museum.*

It is thought that the Warren Tank Car Company fabricated three flats for James Edgar's 1947 Sparks Circus. They looked the same as flats Warren made previously, but comparison to the typical Warrens on either side reveals their shallower depth. *Photograph by George Hubler, 1947, Gift, Dan Smith, Circus World Museum.*

The elephant car of the Dailey Bros. Circus was built by Warren Tank Car Company for Frank West's railroad carnival about 1926. Some elephant cars were built with center or offset doors; others had a pair of them. *Photograph by Art Stensvad, September 28, 1948, North Platte, Nebraska, Circus World Museum.*

A fleet of 25 former U. S. Army hospital cars built by ACF in 1944 were acquired by Ringling Bros. and Barnum & Bailey Combined Shows prior to the 1947 season. Painted red in 1947, they were re-painted aluminum beginning in 1948. *Photograph, June 11, 1949, Upper Darby, Pennsylvania, Gift, Edward J. Pfeiffer, Circus World Museum.*

Elephants were placed in their car side by side, with their heads pointed towards the center of the car. They were backed into this position by their keepers, who then attached their foot chains to rings on the walls or floors. *Photograph by Harry Quillen, 1950, El Monte, California, Circus World Museum.*

The Electro-Motive Division of General Motors built the FTA and FTB diesel-electric road locomotives that the Seaboard Railroad assigned to haul Ringling Bros. and Barnum & Bailey Combined Show's New York train out of quarters. It was making the annual spring run to the important Madison Square Garden engagement. Some of the men are topside, enjoying the last remnants of sunny Florida as the train heads for the colder northern climate. *Print from original negative by Burrell, circa 1949, Howard C. Tibbals Collection.*

The plushness of an owner's private car is evident in this view of one from the Cole Bros. Circus. Though the styling is now dated, at the time it represented the latest of fashion. *Photograph, 1949, Gift, F. Beverly Kelley, Circus World Museum.*

Large numbers of trucks and tractors of various types eliminated the need to use the Barnum show's unloading techniques. Here Case tractor C3 awaits its turn while the D-4 crossing Caterpillar B-1 brings the number 15 menagerie pole wagon down the runs. *Photograph by* Akron Beacon Journal, *July 10, 1949, Akron, Ohio, Circus World Museum.*

The Haffner-Thrall Car Company supplied ten new flats to Ringling Bros. and Barnum & Bailey Combined Shows in 1949 and two more in 1955. These are 1949 models, identifiable by the web splice plates located on the left as one looks straight at the side of the cars. *Photograph by Harold Dunn, 1949, Howard C. Tibbals Collection.*

By the early 1950s all Ringling Bros. and Barnum & Bailey Combined Shows apparatus moved on pneumatic or solid rubber tires, or tracks, giving the show the most modern appearance of any railroad circus. *Print from original negative by Harry Quillen, 1953, Los Angeles, California, Circus World Museum.*

The last railroad circus advertising car was Ringling Bros. and Barnum & Bailey Advertising Car No. 1. It was carefully spotted in advance of a Midwestern date by Chicago and North Western's switch engine number 1262, an Alco S-3 delivered on June 25, 1951. *Photograph, circa 1954, Robert S. MacDougall Collection.*

More Titles from Iconografix:

*This product is sold under license from Mack Trucks, Inc. Mack is a registered Trademark of Mack Trucks, Inc. All rights reserved.

All Iconografix books are available from direct mail specialty book dealers and bookstores worldwide, or can be ordered from the publisher. For book trade and distribution information or to add your name to our mailing list contact:

Iconografix, PO Box 446, Hudson, Wisconsin, 54016 Telephone: (715) 381-9755, (800) 289-3504 (USA), Fax: (715) 381-9756

MORE GREAT BOOKS FROM ICONOGRAFIX

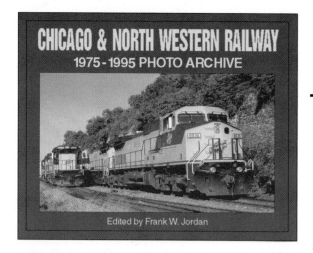

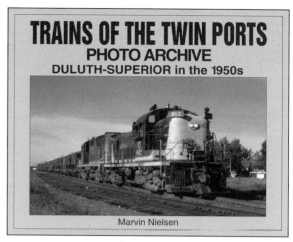

CHICAGO & NORTH WESTERN RAILWAY
1975-1995 Photo Archive
ISBN 1-882256-76-X

TRAINS OF THE TWIN PORTS, DULUTH-SUPERIOR IN THE 1950s Photo Archive
ISBN 1-58388-003-8

WISCONSIN CENTRAL LIMITED 1987-1996 Photo Archive
ISBN 1-882256-75-1

GREAT NORTHERN RAILWAY 1945-1970 Photo Archive
ISBN 1-882256-56-5

CHICAGO, ST. PAUL, MINNEAPOLIS & OMAHA RAILWAY 1880-1940 Photo Archive
ISBN 1-882256-67-0

MILWAUKEE ROAD 1850-1960 Photo Archive
ISBN 1-882256-61-1

SOO LINE 1975-1992 Photo Archive
ISBN 1-882256-68-9

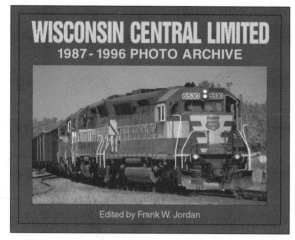

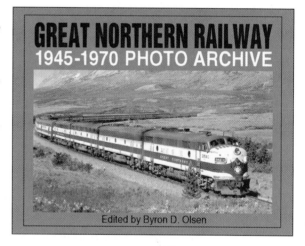

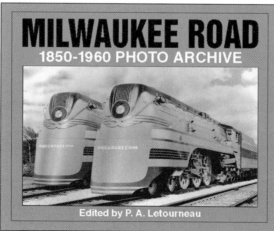